Something
Told Me

Rev. Delores Winfield Edwards

Something Told Me
Copyright © 2020 Rev. Delores Winfield Edwards
Jade Publishing

This book or parts thereof may not be reproduced in any form, stored in a retrieval system, or transmitted in any form by any means – electronic, mechanical, photocopy, recording, or otherwise – without prior written permission of the publisher and author, except as provided by United States of America copyright law.

Unless otherwise indicated, all Scripture quotations are taken from the Holy Bible, Kings James Version, copyright © 1996. Used by permission of Tyndale House Publishers, Inc., Wheaton, Illinois 60189. All rights reserved. Scripture quotations are from The ESV® Bible (The Holy Bible, English Standard Version®), copyright © 2001 by Crossway, a publishing ministry of Good News Publishers. Used by permission. All rights reserved. Scripture taken from the New King James Version. Copyright © 1982 by Thomas Nelson, Inc. Used by permission. All rights reserved." Scripture quotations marked (NLT) are taken from the Holy Bible, New Living Translation, copyright © 1996, 2004, 2007, 2013, 2015 by Tyndale House Foundation. Used by permission of Tyndale House Publishers, Inc., Carol Stream, Illinois 60188. All rights reserved. "Scripture taken from the NEW AMERICAN STANDARD BIBLE®, Copyright © 1960,1962,1963,1968,1971,1972,1973,1975,1977,1995 by The Lockman Foundation. Used by permission. Scriptures taken from the Holy Bible, New International Version®, NIV®. Copyright © 1973, 1978, 1984, 2011 by Biblica, Inc.™ Used by permission of Zondervan. All rights reserved worldwide. www.zondervan.com The "NIV" and "New International Version" are trademarks registered in the United States Patent and Trademark Office by Biblica, Inc.™ "Scripture taken from the NEW AMERICAN STANDARD BIBLE®, Copyright ©1960,1962,1963,1968,1971,1972,1973,1975,1977,1995 by The Lockman Foundation. Used by permission." Scripture quotations marked (GNT) are from the Good News Translation in Today's English Version- Second Edition Copyright © 1992 by American Bible Society. Used by Permission. The American Standard Version (ASV) of the Holy Bible was first published in 1901 by Thomas Nelson & Sons. This translation of the Holy Bible is in the public domain, since its copyright has expired and is the predecessor to the New American Standard Bible.

International Standard Book Number: 978-0-9992591-3-9

First Edition

Printed in the United States of America

us, as he is still doing with Rev. Dee, is one of the exciting mysteries in the walk of faith.

- Robert C. ("Rob") Warren, Jr.
BA in Political Science and English,
Juris Doctor from Howard University
Practicing Attorney 30+ years (Washington, DC)
Proud 40+ year member of Omega Psi Phi
Fraternity, Inc.

Endorsements

This book is a moving and biographical examination of the sixth sense and its curious place in Dee's generational family. Her story comes alive and speaks to our heart about love, family and faith in God. Something Told Me reveals the power and simplicity of God's voice leading us along life's journey. "You will hear a word behind you saying, this is the way: walk in it!" (Isaiah 30:21).

*- Deborah Carter Fontaine, Ph.D,
President & CEO, Re-Imagine Your Future!
Former Vice President, University Advancement,
Norfolk State University*

Something Told Me was a fascinating story arc of how a person's life is often an obstacle course. Rev. Dee's recounting of her life has the same type of whimsical feel that one might get from reading The Color Purple or The Autobiography of Miss Jane Pittman. Through ups and downs, triumphs and tragedies and even bouts with spiritual discernment, Rev. Dee shows that God is always working on us. Allowing God to have his way with

Dedication

This book is dedicated to the awesome family into which I was born. Thank you, James Edward Smith, Jr. (Daddyree) and Nettie Mae Mainor Smith (Mumma). Thank you, William Sylvester Winfield (Granddaddy) and Naomi Brown Winfield (Gramma). Thank you, Vernon Hall Winfield, Sr. (Daddy) and Helen Brett Smith Winfield (Mommie).

My sentiments might best be summed up in a profound truth Daddy shared, at a time in my young adulthood, when I expressed a less than admirable view of his parenting skills. He only responded, "I did the best I could, at the time." My selfish attitude was replaced with gratitude for him and my entire family.

I humbly honor the struggles, the sacrifices, the love, the abounding faith in God and the liberal expressions of their *sixth sense*. Thank you, God!

Table of Contents

"When my heart is overwhelmed: lead me to a rock that is higher than I."
Psalms 61:2b, (KJV)

Foreword

Have you ever thought about what is sometimes called the *sixth sense*? Well, I heard about this *sixth sense* all my life - something more than our five natural senses of taste, touch, smell, hearing, and sight. And yet, it remained a mystery to me until I began to consider what my elders called, "*something told me.*"

In my decision to write this book, I felt it important to share my story of growing up in a wonderful family whose lives appeared to be concentrated with an uncanny sense of awareness and discernment about things that had not yet happened. The common thread was that each of them used the same words to describe it, *something told me*. Not only did my family members use this phrase, but most people I encountered, as I was growing up, whenever they had a "feeling" about a particular situation, they said the same thing. What was the *something* they were feeling? Were they hearing real voices? Was it all in their minds? What were they even talking about? Each of my unanswered questions seemed to compel me to seek for clarity.

For such inquiries, I could only begin at the beginning with my detailed recollections of those abundantly rich family stories. Stories about my maternal grandmother are exceptionally vivid about how she sensed possible difficulties before they became apparent, especially within the family. She called it a 'feeling." I also observed some rather perplexing events regarding my mother who once saved two small children from an unknown fate because of a "feeling" she had. My sister, Joan, seemed to follow suit as her "feeling" propelled her to a dark and anxiety ridden state of mind when she foresaw the death of our maternal grandfather. I vaguely wondered if other families experienced these emotions? No one in my family really talked about it, nor did I ever ask. I think I was afraid of what the answer might be. Although I did not understand the significance of their experiences, I concluded that I would rather not know or experience this "feeling." I could not be sure if it was a gift or an inescapable lifelong burden to bear.

Interestingly, the manifestation of the *sixth sense or something told me,* that I had been avoiding, overtook me when I had my own epiphany when I was seventeen years old. I also realized my family could not be the only people who were experiencing these *feelings* or *sixth sense*. Through this book, I will begin my journey of discovery by telling, not only, my own story and that of my family, but also to find others who wanted to tell their *something told me* stories too.

Acknowledgements

"For from him and through him and to him are all things. To him be glory forever! Amen"

(Romans 11:36, NIV).

Inspiration to write this book, as with all works of art, musical compositions, and the Holy Script, were originated obtained, attained, and achieved through God. I take credit for only the mistakes or missed cues from the Holy Spirit. My heart was always in the right place while the head may have been distracted. I give thanks and glory to God, His Son Jesus Christ, and the Holy Spirit for this manuscript from inception to completion.

I wish to also thank, my husband of 57 years, Rev. Dr. James Edwards, III, for always inspiring me and pushing me towards the finish line. When I was too tired or too alternately project focused, his gentle reminders forced me back on task. He is my greatest cheerleader and amen corner, as well as one of my first draft readers. Thank you, Daddy!

To my friend, Robert C. Warren, Esq., you are simply the best. You were there as my first draft manuscript editor. Without hesitation, you agreed to take time to struggle with me through suggested ideas and grammatical corrections, helping to create order out of my chaos. Although my manuscript arrived water damaged, you labored through the smears and tattered edges and blessed me greatly. Thank you, Rob!

Enough cannot be said about the enormous amount of assistance I received from my talented and gifted friend and sister in Christ, Dr. Deborah Fontaine. I am grateful to God that He led me to ask you to be one of my first draft readers. Your attention to detail, and deliberate focus on reading flow, content clarity, and grammar, helped draw out the best in me while still highlighting with that dreaded red pen. Thank you, Debbie!

Without the generosity and love shown by my friend, sister in Christ, and Historic First Baptist Church member, Frances Brown-Stone, this book would be incomplete. You shared some of your deepest heartbreaks of tragic loss with such candor during our interviews. I am forever grateful for the trust you placed in me to tell your story and share your eternal optimism of faith and trust in Almighty God. Thank you, Frankie!

To Joan Lee Winfield Wilson, who has stood as a matriarchal figure to our sister Deborah, our brother, Vernon and me, all our lives. Thank you for sharing and refreshing my memory during our interviews, as well as providing pictures, names and references that were long since forgotten. Your generosity continues, as the Spirit leads you to be available when He speaks. Thank you, Sis!

Chapter 1

Why Do I Need A Sixth Sense?

As Christians, we believe that our Creator endowed us with five senses: taste, touch, smell, hearing, and sight. Quite conscientiously we experience all five of our senses, daily, if we are so blessed to have them all functioning. If we do have them, we seem to take for granted we will, not only, always have them, but that they will be operating optimally. If we think about it, our five inborn senses are recognized and relied upon without question throughout our lives. Each sense makes it possible for us to survive in a world filled with the pleasures and necessities that each of them brings. How bland and inert our existence would be without our sensory perceptions. To never savor the delightful taste of cinnamon or hazelnut or smell freshly mowed grass after a summer rain or the sweet scent of a playful puppy's breath, diminishes our existence. We soar the heights of pleasure when feeling the warmth of a mother's caress or listen to the melodious harmony of Beethoven, the Beatles, or Beyonce. Little else compares to the spark of love in your sweetheart's eyes or the beauty of a sunset or the brilliance of a sunrise that when absent, renders us void of that essential balance for living the best life. In countless ways our senses help to complete us as human beings.

The sense organs, eyes, ears, nose, tongue, and skin, work together to help us experience a more abundant life as shared in John 10:10b, KJV, "I am come that they might have life and that they might have it more abundantly."

We understand well, why we have five senses. This was an easy lesson learned from grade school. We all can identify readily with each of our five senses and their function. These are natural attributes and there is no disagreement as to their existence or purpose. This knowledge, however, does not bring us any closer to understanding the reason for having a *sixth sense*, especially given that it does not seem to serve the body in the practical ways like taste, touch, smell, hearing and sight do.

I am reminded of a surgery I had many years ago. The doctor informed me that while he was preforming the surgery, he was also going to remove my appendix as it did not really serve a purpose. I wondered what he meant by that. Did God equip us with an organ that served no purpose? Much later, I realized I either missed an important part, or he failed to clarify his rationale. The doctor explained that if my appendix ever became inflamed at some future point, it could pose a major medical dilemma. Obviously, what he was really saying was that the risks of future problems outweighed the need to keep my appendix. This understanding only elicited another question for me regarding our five senses, "What could possibly be the benefit of having an extra sense or *a sixth sense*?"

Let us agree that man is made up of spirit and flesh and was created in God's image. So why wouldn't we be endowed with the same attributes? I believe the *sixth sense* is really a spiritual addendum. It is that part of us that is not rooted in our other five senses but is at the core of our very existence and is just as integral to our wellbeing as the other five natural senses. *"Thus saith God Jehovah, he that created the heavens, and stretched them forth; he that spread abroad the earth and that which cometh out of it; he that giveth breath unto the people upon it, and spirit to them that walk therein"* (Isaiah 42:5 NKJV).

Our feeble attempts at explaining the *sixth sense* fall short because we lack words or references to adequately do so. How do you describe a feeling so everyone can understand? It equates to the doctor asking if the pain is sharp, dull, pinging, deep or shallow when all you know is that it hurts. Try to remember if you have ever tried to describe a moment of great exhilaration and happiness or a great movie. Almost always, the retelling of it rarely rises to the same level as shown in the faces of those with whom you are attempting to describe it. In such cases, your final words might have been, "I guess you just had to be there."

This degree of difficulty in explaining the *instinct, the sight, the feeling, the sixth sense* often merely perpetuates the misunderstanding. I now realize that the Spirit is essential for our understanding of who we are, and more importantly, who God is. Of course, I did not know this when my journey began in understanding about *something told me.*

Chapter 2

We Fear What We Do Not Understand

We all should be able to agree that the natural senses are essential for life, but there is also another sense that can and does cause us a division in opinions. I believe most people seldom think of what is sometimes described as the *sixth sense*. Webster's Dictionary refers to the *sixth sense* as the power of perception, a keen sense of intuition, emotional sense, and/or paranormal psychological phenomena which includes clairvoyance, extrasensory perception, second sight, and psychokinesis. The *sixth sense* is viewed by many as a special ability or power to know something that cannot be learned by using either of the other five natural senses. Parapsychologists have been conducting investigations for evidence of *sixth sense* events for many years.

Before the scientific era and the Age of Enlightenment, stories of unexplained events and unearthly encounters were told and have been passed down from generations to this current day. This type of phenomena has existed from mediums (a familiar spirit at Endor) in the Old Testament (I Samuel 28:7-12), and haunted houses in ancient Greece, to the modern-day television trademark spoon bending illusions of Uri Geller, a self-proclaimed psychic, and the Extrasensory Perception (ESP) abilities of Bob Cassidy, a professional entertainer, who claims to convince any audience he can read their mind.

Wherever mankind has lived, stories shrouded in spooks, specters, magic, and miracles have been part of the culture. These events or encounters were likely manifested first as superstition and folklore, then as unholy and unnatural, or as events that simply lie outside scientific explanation.

During 17th century colonial New England, it was a commonly held belief among the Puritan sect, that Satan gave certain individuals the power to harm others in return for their loyalty. The infamous Salem Witch Trials (1692 –1693) were fueled by suspicions and resentment toward their neighbors, as well as their fear of outsiders and served as a prime example of how fear, ignorance and hysteria can become a catalyst for man's worst inhumanity towards man. In Salem Village, Massachusetts, a group of young girls claimed to be possessed by Satan and proceeded to accuse other women of witchcraft. A wave of panic overshadowed the small town prompting a special court to be convened to try the accused women of witchcraft.

Numerous atrocities were committed against many innocent individuals who were condemned to a fiery death at the stake or a watery demise by drowning. They were judged to be witches and their family members and friends were found to be guilty by association because they were perceived to be different from themselves. Local superstitions generally held in the community provided fodder for the initiation of mass efforts to rid the town of the devil's influence. The fearful town's people seemed determined that the top targets to pursue were the poor, the homeless and most vulnerable residents. From documented reports, the townspeople thought the devil could use this powerless group to do his bidding. In addition, this group was the least likely to be capable of defending themselves against these bogus charges. The court convicted and hung the first person by June of 1692. Eventually, there were one hundred and fifty more men, women, and children accused of witchcraft. The lesson learned from the Salem story is that we fear what we do not understand.

Oftentimes, we respond to fear with suspicion, distrust, animosity, or hate, which are common human susceptibilities. When afraid, we look for support for the angst we feel toward often-unfounded terrors of "things that go bump in the night". The earliest recorded use of this particular phrase was 1918 in the *Bulletin of the School Oriental and African Studies*:

> *"To a people ... who ... believe in genii, ghosts, goblins, and those terrific things that 'go bump in the night', protective charms are eagerly sought for."*

> *"Things that go bump in the night.*
> *From ghoulies and ghosties*
> *And long-leggedy beasties*
> *And things that go bump in the night,*
> *Good Lord, deliver us!"*

Because we cannot seem to fathom what the "bump in the night" is, we tend to fear the invisible noise in the dark and imagine it is something that has come to harm us.

Typically, in trying to figure out what things mean, we seek for a logical explanation or reputable source for confirmation. When we feel that something does not fit into our way of thinking, in a way we can make sense of it we may resort to inserting our sometimes, irrational theories much like the township in Salem, Massachusetts at the Salem Witch Trials, or the invisible bump in the night. Our imagination attempts to force fit its meaning or create a basis to help put us at ease. The bump in the night might be seen more clearly in the morning, as an unlatched shutter blown back and forth against the house by the wind and not an evil spirit.

We seek for answers that validate our assessment and aid us in our effort to make sense of what we do not understand. To this end, we sometimes try to force information to fit our own level of understanding. This is done to make sure that the "square peg" (our imagination/our ideas/our fears) force fit themselves into the "round hole" (reality/truth). In other words, our misguided thinking can be used to give credence to whatever narrative a person wishes to convey.

An illustration of force fitting a "square peg into a round hole" can be amplified by a term used in scriptural study that expresses the interpreter's own thoughts, ideas, and biases. The term is *eisegesis* and it is a process that twists the textual truth to match ones thinking. This process takes information out of context and substitutes a subjective interpretation that confirms a personal opinion or perspective, which is not necessarily reality or truth. The same can be said for eisegesis of philosophy, justice, morals, ethics, etc., that result in the promotion and profiteering of others by merely adhering to the parts he or she likes best.

There are those who seek to confirm the suitability of fortunetellers, mediums, familiar spirits, tarot card and crystal ball reading, and have been known to refer to the Bible as their supporting example despite the Bible's express warning denouncing such practices. *"Let no one be found among you who sacrifices their son or daughter in the fire, who practices divination or sorcery, interprets omens, engages in witchcraft, or casts spells, or who is a medium or spiritist or who consults the dead"* (Deuteronomy 18:10-11, NIV). We fear what we do not understand.

Chapter 3

Frankie's Something Told Me Moments

A wonderful woman named Frances "Frankie" Brown-Stone was feared by her friends because they did not understand the *sixth sense* she displayed. Some of them stopped having close relationships with her because they feared what she might perceive about them. This decline in close friendships caused her to retreat, for a period of time, into obscurity.

When I met Frankie in 2014, I felt a kindred spirit at our first meeting. We knew one another casually by way of membership at the same church, Historic First Baptist Church, Norfolk, Virginia. Frankie was always very warm with a quick inviting smile. She was also very forthright and funny. It was not until she came to a grief support group I was facilitating, that I got to know her on a different level. Frankie shared in our group session that she and her sisters, Dot and Pearl, were very close. Dot died and shortly afterward, Pearl died. Coupled with the death of Frankie's daughter and a granddaughter, she found it difficult coping with the void they left and sought help. The sisters were inseparable...whether at church gatherings, chatting daily or as traveling road buddies. As her time in grief support continued, Frankie began to share some of her personal experiences with what she called, *the sight* or *mother wit*. My interest was instantly piqued as I contemplated requesting time to interview her for inclusion in this book.

My first interview with Frankie was November 13, 2018 by telephone. We met in person on several other occasions as well. She was consistently excited to share her experiences and especially happy to know that others might be blessed by hearing them. Although it was difficult at times for her to relive her experiences, she was fearless and shared from the heart. Frankie Brown-Stone shared her *something told me* moments like a made for television series. Her story revealed her profound and powerful presentation of *the sight or sixth sense.*

During my interview with Frankie, she shared how she was somewhat of an "outcast" and was treated (in her words) as a "freak of the week" because of her *sixth sense* or special ability. Adapting herself to operate in a way that was acceptable to those around her...always making sure others did not feel uncomfortable became a priority for Frankie, regardless of her own personal pain surrounding her *sixth sense.*

Frankie Brown-Stone shared an eye-opening scenario that painfully described examples of how she was made to feel she was an outsider. As Frankie began her story, she shared that friends would invite her to visit their friends and loved ones in the hospital because they knew Frankie could envision, what Frankie referred to as, the "death mask." She explained this term was used by her mother, indicating that a person's death was imminent. Because of this awareness, Frankie began to shy away from going to the hospital with people. After all, it was not as if she took pleasure in this revelation or had any desire to experience this phenomenon repeatedly. As a matter of fact, she would, not only see the "death mask" but also experience physical symptoms of body weakness and heart palpitations. She was in such agony, at times, she was not able to work. She hated seeing the look on the faces of her friends as they watched her in the hospital room with their loved ones. Frankie's friends and colleagues displayed a mixture of fear and awe at her ability. Nobody likes a "know it all," Frankie said. This quote has a quirk in the reference this time because it refers to people who fear others who know what they do not. The scope of the *sixth sense* is not limited to a particular modality or way in which it presents itself. Frankie could perceive the "death mask" on dying people. She knew when a person's death was imminent. The *sight* was manifested sometimes by way of her dreams and at other times spiritual discernment.

While God is consistent in His intervention in our lives, He does not always use the same process or instructional specifics. Consider, the difference between God's instruction to Moses in (Exodus 17:6, NIV), *"I will stand there before you by the rock at Horeb. Strike the rock, and water will come out of it for the people to drink"* and (Numbers 20:8b, NIV), *"Speak to that rock before their eyes and it will pour out its water."* Today, His manifestation may be repackaged...we may not have a rock to strike or speak to in the desert but, like Moses, we must attune ourselves with His Spirit via our *sixth sense.* *"Jesus Christ is the same yesterday, today and forever (Hebrews 13:8, NIV).*

Too often, our fears instruct our attitudes, ideas, and behaviors rather than knowledge of the truth. Frankie assumed that people probably wondered or internally questioned if she might be telepathic or able to read their mind? Does Frankie have foresight, can she tell my future? If people possess the power to see and know the things that are not present, what horrible, unimaginable crimes might Frankie be able to inflict upon me? Am I exposed and vulnerable because someone possibly knows something about me, I have not told them? A natural inclination might be to identify the person with the *sixth sense* as a threat that must be silenced by ridicule or even ruin. Sadly, Frankie became aware very early in her life what an exhausting and lifelong effort it is to hide a natural part of yourself.

Frankie says she does not remember a time when she did not have very vivid dreams that held deep meaning for future events or experiences of what her mother also called, *the sight.*

One such experience was a certain recurring dream that was very troubling to Frankie because she would wake up crying while experiencing terrible pain in her chest...her heart just seemed to hurt. She finally told her sister, Pearl, about it. Pearl suggested that the next time Frankie had the dream that she should force herself to stay in the dream. The next time the familiar dream returned, Frankie was walking, once again, down a hospital corridor where she felt intense heat. In the dream, she saw someone who was wrapped in a blanket from head to toe. There were other people in the hallway but suddenly, in the dream, Frankie knew that one of those people "belonged" to her. She exclaimed, "Oh my God, that's my baby." While continuing to walk down the hospital corridor, Frankie's daughter changed direction and entered a different hallway. Frankie awoke wondering what it all meant.

Three months later, at 41 years old, her daughter, Taitsia (pronounced Tot-she a), was diagnosed with a rare extremely painful medical condition called Stevens-Johnson Syndrome/toxic epidural necrolysis. This condition is a reaction triggered by a medication or an infection like pneumonia or herpes virus. This disease presents as flu-like symptoms followed by blisters on the body and often includes blisters on the mucous membranes. A rash develops that causes the skin to die (necrosis) and detach. Patients diagnosed with this disease are treated in the ICU, Dermatology or Burn unit. Taitsia was admitted to the burn unit in an induced coma. Although her daughter was in an induced coma, every day when she and her sister, Dot, visited, Taitsia always made movements of some kind, as if somehow, she knew her mother was near.

Since Taitsia was in an unconscious state, Frankie was not sure if her daughter sensed her presence or Frankie just hoped she could. The doctors told her that Taitsia could possibly hear her speak. How her daughter could detect the difference in the nurse approaching or her mother approaching was always a bit puzzling to Frankie. Frankie wondered if, somehow, Taitsia, knew her scent or perceived her faint footsteps entering the Burn Unit? Was it possible for Taitsia's other senses to now be heightened to the point that she could recognize her mother's inaudible heartbeat? Frankie knew Taitsia was dying but her desire was to hold her daughter close and preserve their intense mother-daughter relationship that was shared from the womb for as long as possible. It is not for me to confirm or deny what Frankie felt. I can only speculate. Taitsia was in a state of medically induced coma and though she appeared to be asleep, her brain was not. She was aware...she knew.

Frankie did not perceive Taitsia's response to her, while in a coma, as confirmation that the *sixth sense* existed but as a sign of a continued love connection between them. There was a stark similarity between the dream and the living nightmare she was enduring. The heat in the dream mimicked the awful disease that caused Taitsia to be admitted to the burn unit and Frankie's daughter was wrapped in full sterile dressing in the burn unit. Despite the fact that the dream was a horrific premonition of what was to come, Frankie says her faith in an Almighty God demanded she accept His will. She shared that her mother, grandmother, and her Aunt Alberta were also amazing women of God who shared this ability they all referred to as *the sight or mother wit*. Based on this premise, every generation has an obligation to pass on the fact that this *sixth sense* is a blessing from God and to be cherished, not feared or ridiculed. *"Therefore, my beloved brethren, be ye steadfast, unmovable, always abounding in the work of the Lord,"* (I Corinthians 15:58 a,b, KJV).

Chapter 4

From Generation To Generation

Every generation learns from the previous one. However, each generation wants to feel they are forward thinking and can choose the traditions and beliefs they will retain or discard. The responsibility for reminding the next generation does not change. *"We will not hide them from their descendants; we will tell the next generation the praiseworthy deeds of the Lord, his power, and the wonders he has done (Psalm 78:4, NIV).* Every tool God has placed in their toolboxes, including the *sixth sense*, must be used for righteous living that will benefit the people and bring glory to God.

There are many false impressions regarding those who experience this *sixth sense, instinct, feeling, or the sight.* I now realize it is not a mistake in nature or an anomaly to be feared. The *sixth sense* is not a foreign object, abnormal growth, or painful abscess that should be excised from the body, but it is to be fully embraced through vigilance, diligence, and observance to God's glory. By appropriately using the word of God, the distinction between what is real and what is imagined becomes crystal clear. Our Christian doctrines are based on the belief that from the first generation, God spoke the world into existence and breathed life into man and created him in His image (Genesis 1:27). I would submit that God endowed us with all six senses "in the beginning."

Throughout my life, I have been very aware of the presence of the *sixth sense* in my family generations. My maternal grandmother, Nettie Mae Mainor Smith, my mother, Helen Brett Smith Winfield, my sister, Joan Lee Winfield Wilson, and my friend, Frances Brown-Stone, and I have all experienced the manifestation of God's Spirit. I cannot say with confidence that we always knew that it was God's Spirit, because if we did, perhaps we would not have referred to it as *"Something told me,"* but more aptly as, *"the Spirit told me."*

The family stories that follow will attest that my relatives were and are just ordinary people trying to live the life God gave them. There are some situations, events, and occurrences that can be corroborated but cannot be literally explained.

My mother's side of the family seemed to be average folks, in my opinion. There always seemed to be nuggets of stories shared in lighthearted conversation by my mother. She recalled a time during the 1920s Jim Crow Virginia when my grandmother, whom we called, Mumma, took my mother downtown to shop using public transportation. The bus driver assumed that Mumma was a white woman and insisted she ride in the front of the bus... but the little curly haired, dimpled, mulatto child holding her hand would have to go to the back. They both got off the bus and walked. I do not know if this was the last time Mumma used public transportation, but I never knew her to do her own personal in-person shopping while I was growing up. Mumma's younger sister, Aunt Josie, enjoyed using public transportation as an opportunity to ride comfortably. Aunt Josie walked far enough outside the perimeter of her segregated community in Huntersville to catch a bus. She too, was mistaken for a white woman but the difference was that Aunt Josie never bothered to correct the driver. She took her seat at the front and rode all the way downtown. When Aunt Josie got off the bus, she shopped where she wanted to and tried on the latest fashions including hats (without covering her head with a plastic bag, as was the customary requirement for Black people). She also went to the white beauty salons for her hair appointments. As the story goes, "passing" for white was always a point of contention between Mumma and Aunt Josie. However, they seemed to be reconciled on most other matters and had a great time in the retelling of it.

My grandmother was a "stay at home mom" long before the term slipped into our modern-day cultural vocabulary. She was "just" a housewife or homemaker. Although I was told she had teaching credentials which she earned while attending Old Mission College in Norfolk, Virginia, I was never aware that she ever used them. As the family story goes, Mumma tried to help someone get a job and gave them her teaching credentials to use. When Mumma married my grandfather, James Edward Smith, Sr., it was not customary for married women to teach and it was expected, particularly in the mid 1900s, that she would settle in to raise a family. My grandfather, James Edward Smith, Jr. (Daddyree) would be the "breadwinner." He retired as a pullman porter with the Norfolk and Western Railroad and later retired as a mail carrier for the U.S. Post Office. These jobs enabled him to provide a middle-class lifestyle for his family and purchase their home on Johnson Avenue in Norfolk.

My grandmother came from a prominent Black family that included her grandfather, Rev. Rufus Mainor and her father, Rev. John J. Mainor (1864-1934) and her stepmother, Alice Jeffries Mainor. Mumma's mother, Josephine, died when she was twenty-seven years old, leaving my grandmother, Nettie, her sister, Josephine, and brother Johnnie heartbroken. Her father remarried and her half brothers and sisters included Rufus, Eugenia, Helen Brett and Dorothy Leigh Mainor. "Papa", as my grandmother referred to her father, was the pastor of several churches in Norfolk. St John's AME

Church was where our family and I attended church. I vaguely remember hearing that "PaPa" or "Papa Grand" as my New York cousins referred to him, was a preacher and that his father was a Methodist minister. Mumma's siblings that I knew, included her brother (Uncle John "Johnnie" Mainor) her sister (Aunt Josephine "Josie" Mainor Nixon Whitley), and Aunt Helen Brett Coleman-Scott), who was a half-sister who lived in St. Albans, Queens, New York. The youngest half-sister (Dorothy Leigh (Mainor) Maynor) was an internationally acclaimed concert singer in the 1940s-1960s. Mumma's other siblings included a half-sister (Aunt Eugenia) and half-brother (Uncle Rufus Reginald Mainor). I did not get to know my grandmother's siblings, except for Aunt Josie and her second husband, Riley, and her child from her first marriage to Uncle "Nick", (Aunt Thomasine "Tommie" Nixon Pruden) and her children. I did not get to know Uncle Johnnie and his wife, Aunt Malvene and family very well, until I was almost grown and took my children to visit them on East Lexington Street in Norfolk. Periodically, I would wonder why this part of my family seemed to be a bit disconnected and did not seem to communicate with each other very much, although Mumma, Aunt Josie, and Uncle Johnnie went to St. John's AME church and lived in the same city. I was glad this was not the case with Mumma and Daddyree when it came to our immediate family.

Most Sundays were a special time when my parents and siblings all went to St John's church together and I always sat with Mumma and Daddyree. Daddyree was not very tall but he was very stout and sang with great gusto. He noticed one Sunday that I was not singing and asked me why? I replied that I did not know the words. I remember him telling me to move my lips, listen to the music, and soon I would know all the songs by heart. He was right. After service we would gather at our grandparents' home for the great family feast.

My grandparent's spacious home on Johnson Avenue in the Huntersville section of Norfolk holds precious memories of kitchen aromas of fresh baked goodies and church music. Mumma played the great hymns on the piano at home. She loved opera and classical music which was the music from her childhood. Another favorite of hers was the televised Billy Graham Crusades. During those revivals, Mumma's tears never failed to flow when gospel artist, George Beverly Shea sang "How Great Thou Art." Daddyree played beautiful hymns, as well, but also the magnificent sounds of John Phillip Sousa on trumpet. He played in the brass section as a member of the African American community's beloved Excelsior Band, established in 1881. I remember as a child, running alongside the band on Church Street during our community Independence Day parades. They wore light brown uniforms with matching hats. My grandfather's eyes twinkled as he winked at us while playing his trumpet. He would sweat profusely. I could not be sure if he was sweating more because of the fourth of July heat or his rotund body marching in step in that slightly snug heavy weight uniform.

There always seemed to be endless delights experienced at my grandparent's home. My mother's older brother, James Edward Smith, III, was a merchant seaman and added to my grandmother's jewelry chest of beloved treasures. Her love for the items was more about the giver than the gift. He brought home swashbuckling tales and a taste of countries across the globe of silk scarves, porcelain dolls, fine jewelry, and an array of handmade broches on each return trip home.

We were blessed to be exposed so early in life to an appreciation of God, music, literature, poetry, and lots of love which were quite palpable. What was not quite so obvious, but ever present was the underlying discernment that could and did manifest itself at any given moment. It was not unusual to hear family stories shared in this wonderful home about the *sixth sense* and the experiences of my grandmother and my mother.

Chapter 5

Finding Uncle Howard

I remember hearing Mommie telling my siblings and me that her mother had a *sixth sense*. She seemed to always get a "feeling" when something was just not right. She said her mother explained it as an "uneasy feeling." It was at one of these times, my mother said my grandmother asked her to come over to pick her up. Although Mumma died when I was fifteen in 1961, I never knew her to drive a car. When my mother arrived at Mumma's house, she was waiting on the porch clad in a starched cotton print dress, small straw hat, purse, and white gloves. Mumma let her know they were going to search for her oldest son, Howard, who they had not seen for several months. They knew he would be in an area of Norfolk where people, who frankly, if they did not have to live there, would not be there either. Mumma was determined that she had to find her son who had been an alcoholic since he was fifteen years old. Though he was now a grown man, Mumma's instincts about him remained strong. She and my mother walked arm in arm through back alleys and the cobblestone ways of Chicazola Street, Smith Street, Wide Street, and Henry Street, asking where she could find her son. Since these were familiar haunts for Uncle Howard, most people knew him. They also knew my grandmother because this was not her first trip to these places of despair and desolation in the 1950s post World War II era.

The two women spent hours roaming around in the narrow lanes of the most impoverished areas of Norfolk. They were not afraid. Although the neighborhoods were poor, they seemed to show regard for the five-foot one-inch lady who looked like a white woman and the curly-haired young lady who accompanied her. Residents may have been a bit more accepting of this out of place duo from across town as harmless because they were merely looking for someone they loved. Every soul can probably identify with their plight. Even the wino sitting on the curb tipped his hat to them. My mother urged Mumma to return home, emphasizing that Howard would eventually come back as he always did, but she refused. By now it was getting dark and just as my mother was about to suggest again that they leave for home, a figure appeared on a dimly lit porch. Mumma spotted her son stumbling out of a bootlegger's house. Immediately Mumma said, *"Something told me to keep looking and I would find him."* When they got to him, they could see that he had recently been involved in a fight of some kind and found later that some men had beaten him, thinking to rob him. My grandmother took him home without any resistance from Uncle Howard. She tended to his wounds, fed him, and treated him like royalty for at least the few weeks that he would stay. I remember my Uncle Howard as the sweetest drunk I ever knew, who, next to wine, loved the taste of a slice of sharp cheese melting as he dipped it into a hot cup of coffee.

What was it that caused my grandmother to feel this sudden urgency to find her son? Why had she not felt compelled to go find him a week earlier or a month earlier or even some time in the future? I do not claim to know the answer, but my heart tells me this foresight of urgency or *sixth sense* presented itself to Mumma when the need was the greatest. In the book titled, *When God Speaks* by Henry Blackaby and Richard Blackaby, they declare that "God is always speaking but we are not always listening." Our *sixth sense* is there yet we are not always mindful of it or listening to His voice. I would submit to you the plausibility that the mind is so wired by our Creator that He can only speak to some of us when we are not interrupting? We recognize God does not need, as we do, lungs, vocal cords, a larynx, teeth, lips, or a tongue to speak to His creation. He speaks to us by His Spirit. At one time God may converse in a still small voice or a whisper. He may communicate to us via a thought, or a sensation.

There are numerous instances in the Bible where God used the wind, an earthquake, or even a fire to communicate. Some may feel, God used these incredible effects as last resort to make human contact, but these are merely examples of how God chooses to speak to us. Consider that Jesus spoke with a loud voice from the Cross (parallel Gospels of Matthew, Mark, and Luke) or God's voice heard by Moses from above the mercy-seat (Numbers 7:89) connects to the heart with greater power. I believe God can use His still small voice because He is always near...attuned to our life's condition. It was the same still small voice to which my grandmother responded just as my mother would years later.

Chapter 6

Mommie's Something Told Me Moment

When I was a youngster, I was not sure what that uneasy, strange *"something"* was that I overheard in "grown folks" conversation, but it appears that my grandmother was not the only one who experienced this *sixth sense* sensation. My mother underwent her share of *something told me moments,* too. During the late 1950s, I remember my mother sharing that she had a similar "feeling" like the one that Mumma had regarding Uncle Howard. Ironically, her "feeling" was regarding him, too.

It was a frigid January or February evening when my mother asked Daddy to go with her to find Uncle Howard. Once again, somewhere in the impoverished parts of Norfolk, they drove around for a while trying to find someone who knew where he was currently living. After several hours, someone finally referred them to an upstairs apartment in the neighborhood. To their dismay, they found the apartment door ajar and two small children inside, but no sign of Uncle Howard or the children's mother. The apartment had no food and no heat and if it had not been for my parents, it is likely the children would never have survived the night. Immediately my mother sent Daddy to retrieve some old blankets from the trunk of the car. They wrapped the baby girl and her older sister in blankets and brought them to our home in the Crestwood section of Chesapeake, Virginia. Upon their arrival, my mother quickly ordered my siblings and me to get some bathwater ready and to get some of our undershirts and big safety pins. Over the next few days, my father literally gave the shirts off his back, as that were cut up and used as diapers for the new arrival until we could buy more. The two children lived with us for several weeks and we doted on them, as if they belonged to our family until their mother sobered up enough to retrieve them. Mommie did not find Uncle Howard that night but was *sent* to save two very frightened, abandoned children from an uncertain fate. In those days, the social services department never got involved unless there was no one to care for and house the children. If my mother knew about a need, she would just make room. She made room for Uncle Howard's son, Howard, Jr. when his parents (Uncle Howard and Aunt Mariah "Skeeter" Rainey Smith) divorced. Howard Jr.'s sister Rosemary went to live with Aunt Skeeter's sister Mary and husband Will Berry. Today, accepting family members into one's home to live, without financial, physical, or moral support, might appear unusual but to accept a needy non-family member would be the exception.

From the time slaves were brought to America, taking care of each other was a culturally common occurrence for the mutual survival of the race. I can clearly recall witnessing this same behavior in the families in my neighborhood where I grew up. Our neighbors across the street had a family of nine children and their mother brought her ailing mother to live with them until her death. The entire family took care of Grandma. One of my neighbor's mother died and without hesitation, she raised her three brothers together with her own three children. During our time together in high school, I never realized, until much later, that they were not siblings. Black families took the Bible literally when it espoused, *"Anyone who does not provide for their relatives, and especially for their own household, has denied the faith and is worse than an unbeliever"* (1 Timothy 5:8, NIV). Caring for each other was a powerful biblical principal that was exemplified and interwoven in the fabric of Black American culture. It would have been a stain on a family's reputation to allow an elderly or ailing parent or family member to be cared for in an institution. Welfare of the family was preeminent. I remember my father telling us that he and his sister, Aunt Thalia, were sent to live with relatives in Petersburg, Virginia because there was not a high school in Surry that allowed black students to attend. It was all about family connection and provision. Obviously, modeling affectionate, compassionate, and loving behavior in any culture is an enduring factor and its efficacy is measured by the fruit that each generation bears. My siblings and I were beneficiaries of Mommie's model of generosity and gift of helps, as well as the same well used *sixth sense* that her mother displayed.

Chapter 7

Joan Lee's Something Told Me Moments

...And the fruit did not fall very far from the tree. A family trait seemed to be repeating itself and penetrating yet another generation. First my grandmother, then my mother, and now, Joan. My oldest sister, Joan Lee Winfield Wilson, was always very intelligent, creative, and very serious about almost everything. As the oldest sibling her responsibility was to nurture her three younger siblings and our cousin, Howard, Jr. As we grew older, she got up in the mornings and made sure we had breakfast before school. She was cognizant of the whereabouts of each of us at any given time... if by chance, my parents should ask. What I did not become aware of until Joan Lee was in her early twenties was that she too had the *sixth sense*.

Yes, it was the same sense of uneasiness, my grandmother and my mother experienced.

By 1963, Uncle Howard had been an alcoholic for about thirty-eight years. His family loved and supported him as much as they could. My grandmother's *sixth sense* sent her on a number of missions to help and rescue him while she lived. After she died, my mother, though she was fifteen years younger than Uncle Howard, received the baton from her mother to safeguard his welfare as best she could.

Mommie and Daddy moved to Long Island, New York in 1963 when Daddy received orders to change duty stations while serving in the Navy. My mother was somewhat concerned that she would no longer be physically close enough to Uncle Howard to maintain that watchful eye over him. However, she felt some relief because Joan Lee would now become her eyes and ears in Norfolk.

Joan Lee had been aware of all the efforts the family employed to be available for Uncle Howard and understood well what Mommie must be feeling. Although Joan saw Uncle Howard infrequently, she knew the general vicinity of where he lived.

Joan was training as a phlebotomist while working at Norfolk Community Hospital (Colored people) in Norfolk. She was living at 763 Johnson Avenue in the Huntersville section of Norfolk with our grandfather, Daddyree, after Mumma died in 1962 due to heart failure. Joan had gotten married in June of 1963 and was working while her husband, Duward, was deployed in the Navy.

The night before Uncle Howard died, Joan had a dream that Uncle Howard was lying on a blue sofa. In the dream, Uncle Howard nearly died...he had a "knot" in his stomach and told God, "I don't want to hurt like this." In her dream, Uncle Howard went to sleep. Joan Lee awoke the next morning and remembered the details of the dream but wondered why she was dreaming about something so morbid. The next evening the man with whom Uncle Howard had been rooming, contacted Daddyree to let him know his son, Howard Lee Smith, Sr. had died. When Daddyree shared the details that Uncle Howard's roommate gave, Joan Lee was amazed at how much the details paralleled her dream. According to the roommate, Uncle Howard was working again and decided to stretch out on the sofa after dinner. His roommate later went to bed, assuming Uncle Howard would do so later. The next morning, the roommate left very early to go to work and noticed Uncle Howard had slept on the sofa all night but did not feel concerned. It was only when he returned home when he saw that Uncle Howard was in the same position as when he left for work that he realized

Uncle Howard had died on the sofa in the living room. The coroner attributed his death to a heart attack in his sleep the night before. Joan's *sixth sense* had revealed Uncle Howard's impending death in her dream.

Mommie and Daddy came home from Long Island, New York and her sister Gladys came from Lorain, Ohio to attend Uncle Howard's funeral. Mommie told us that God did not have to "find" Uncle Howard as Mumma, she and Joan had done so many times before. He knew where he was and took him home to be with Him. Mommie would no longer have to keep her promise to my grandmother and she was now released from guardianship of her brother each time *something told her* to go find him.

It would only be another eight years that Mommie lived to share her generosity with all of us. I was twenty-five when Mommie died of a massive heart attack on September 26, 1971 at the age of forty-four which was also my daughter, Donita's, fifth birthday. Mommie touched many lives in the short time she lived while those of us who are given more time seem to accomplish so much less. Daddy used to say that Mommie was always picking up strays. Her heart seemed always big enough to include raising the four of us and later our cousin, Howard, Jr., several homeless dogs, a fawn, numerous unrelated needy children, and many racially diverse desperate adults. It would take another book to share all my memories of the treasure trove of souls that filled our home during my childhood. I believe she was motivated by the love of God and a heart for the less fortunate, as well as family, sprinkled with an abundance of *something told me* moments.

Joan's dream and the actual account of Uncle Howard's death was very unsettling for her. Little did she know that it would not be very long before she would have yet another, *something told me moment.* Her next *sixth sense* experience would far surpass the intensity of what she felt regarding Uncle Howard.

In February 1965, Joan was living, once again, with Daddyree while her husband, was deployed. Daddyree was happy to have his beloved oldest granddaughter's company in the empty house that was filled with so many memories. Joan worked her off-circadian rhythm schedule of the midnight shift at the hospital. She said her natural sleep pattern never adjusted to nighttime alertness and daytime sleep. Joan Lee was asleep when Daddyree left to go his granddaughter's school event at Campostella Elementary School that evening. When she woke up at about 6:30 p.m., she said she suddenly felt a *sense of uneasiness.* She could not quite put her finger on the feeling, but it was all consuming. By

7:00 p.m., the feeling began to surface as a sense of anxiety peppered with dread. Joan Lee only knew that the feeling had something to do with Daddyree. This happened in 1965 before there were cell phones or means of contacting people other than a street telephone booth or private home phone. Joan began to call the Norfolk hospitals to see if Daddyree had been admitted. She first called Community Hospital where she worked, then she called DePaul Hospital, then Norfolk General Hospital, but to no avail. Joan decided to start calling each hospital back to inquire about him. Joan Lee had no idea why she felt so anxious yet so sure that something bad had happened to Daddyree. Joan continued her systematic calling of each hospital and finally when she called Norfolk General Hospital back, the emergency room confirmed that James Edward Smith, Jr. had been pronounced dead upon arrival.

He was the victim of a hit and run accident only two blocks from home at the traffic light intersection of Church Street and Brambleton Avenue. Later that evening, the police officer on the scene, thought Daddyree was not injured. Daddyree continued to sit behind the wheel of his black 1954 Pontiac Sedan. The officer said when he asked him how he was doing, Daddyree said, "I'm fine... I'm just going to rest my head on the steering wheel for a minute." Daddyree did not die of his injuries, his heart just stopped. All that Joan could say or think was, *"Something told me."*

Chapter 8

I Don't Want It, You Can Have It...It's Too Much For Me

Looking back over my family's experiences with the *sixth sense*, an emerging undeniable insight began to surface. That uneasy, apprehensive, anxious feeling each of them expressed was not what I wanted to be a part of. I would think to myself that I had absolutely no desire to know, see, or feel anything ahead of the time something was to happen. SURPRISE ME! I'll take "shocked out of my gourd" anytime as opposed to cold sweats for some unknown reason. I never remembered hearing anyone in the family say they just LOVED to get that uneasy, almost sick to your stomach feeling that was not brought on by influenza or some disagreeable morsel consumed the night before. Whatever the mystery was surrounding this *sixth sense*, my favorite refrain became, "I don't want it; you can have it; it's too much for me." This was also a popular line from a 1920s blues song by Jelly Roll Martin and later a 1947 Polka hit song by Arthur Godfrey, *I Don't Want Her, You Can Have Her, She's Too Fat For Me.* This quip was my way of brushing off any personal acceptance or recognition of what I now know was the inevitable... I also had a sixth sense. Obviously, the *something told me* phenomenon does *not* necessarily actively operate in families unless you are referring to every person in the entire human race family. These stories may sound bizarre and more like an episode out of the Twilight Zone, but if you think about it, you have probably experienced, to some degree, at least one *something told me moment,* too.

Have you ever made a last-minute decision to change your route home for some "unknown" reason? Later, you found out there was a horrific accident that caused traffic to back up for miles on your usual route. Has it ever crossed your mind to go to a restaurant you had not been to in years, only to find that someone who had been on your mind recently was there too? Perhaps you had an event like mine when I went for a job interview in 1973 at Sentara Norfolk General Hospital in Norfolk, Virginia.

After an introduction and some small talk during my first encounter with a young woman named Carolyn Majette in 1973, she asked if I might be interested in a job at Sentara Norfolk General Hospital. She was the first African American telephone operator hired at the hospital and was moving from the area which would open up a job opportunity. Carolyn told me to go to the hospital and apply for the position as soon as possible because the entry level jobs filled quickly. When I arrived at the Human Resources Department the next day, to my amazement, I saw someone working there who I knew. Her name was Edith Shands Churchill. After we exchanged greetings, and I completed the application, Edith escorted me to the second floor Communications Department. She introduced me to the supervisor and submitted my application. I was surprised when Edith began to praise my attributes and painted a glowing picture of me as potentially the greatest asset to the department in its history and declared it would be a feather in the supervisor's cap if she hired me. That day, I became the second African American telecommunications operator to work at Sentara Norfolk General Hospital. I will always be thankful to Edith for going above and beyond her job responsibilities to help a friend. Oddly, a year after I was hired, my supervisor, Hilda, accused me of not being honest about having had previous experience when I was hired. There was no supporting evidence for such an accusation. I felt sure Hilda was only upset because Edith had praised my employment value so eloquently that Hilda hired me without reading my application thoroughly. One thing was for sure...I now had experience. I remained employed at that hospital for thirteen years.

Could these events have been just coincidences, flukes, or happenstances? Your first thought was probably like mine, *"Something told me* not to go home the usual way, *something told me* to go to that particular restaurant that evening, or *something told me* to apply for that job at the recommendation of a "chance" encounter with a stranger." This was a *something told me moment* for me. One of the cardinal Christian principles teaches that nothing happens by chance, or randomly, or out of control. God is sovereign and everything happens for a reason. Although we are free to operate in this universe, His purposes remain hidden from us and God's Divine Providence, His will, supersedes all others. I believe our *sixth sense* is the means by which the Spirit of God connects with ours to guide us into His purpose for our good. "*In whom also we were made a heritage, having been foreordained according to the purpose of him who worketh all things after the counsel of his will*" (Ephesians 1:11, ASV).

Chapter 9

From Down On The Farm To The Upper Room

Great minds continue to make attempts at harnessing and connecting the dots to come up with reasonable explanations for or against the existence of a *sixth sense*. I can only add context to the debate by sharing my first remembered experience when I was four or five years old at my paternal grandparents' home in Surry, Virginia.

My immediate family lived in the city of Norfolk. Vast amounts of time were spent on the farm in Surry, Virginia, 112 RFD (Rural Free Delivery), during my formative childhood years. In addition to regular visits to the farm during the year, my siblings and I spent every summer and winter school break with my grandparents. My reflections conjure up, wonderful feeling, sights, sounds, and smells of vivid life-long lessons. My grandparents, Deacon William Sylvester Winfield and Deaconess Naomi Brown Winfield were upstanding pillars of the community. They were born and raised in the same county, raised their children, and attended Mount Nebo Baptist Church. Later my siblings and I became part of the fabric of Surry. Everyone knew who we were and embraced us as Willie and Naomi's grandchildren.

Our time at the country, as we referred to Surry, helped establish an exceptional work ethic and a deep-rooted belief that we are our brother's keeper. During planting or harvest season in the spring or hog killing season in the winter, every other Black farmer helped their neighbors to make sure they survived the sometimes harsh and uncertain weather patterns that could make or break their livelihood. Even after my dad, Vernon, and his siblings, Alvin, Thalia, Ward and Nettie, were grown with families of their own, they left their jobs in other states to return to the farm to lovingly do their part. My siblings, Joan Lee, Deborah, and Vernon, Jr., and I, were the only grandchildren until our little cousin, Alvin Winfield, Jr., came along. Much later, our twin cousins, Neva and Nita Mensia, and much later Kimberly Winfield joined the ranks.

My siblings and I worked hard on the farm, helping tend the garden, feeding chickens, gathering eggs, plucking chickens for the next day's meal, weeding peanuts, churning butter, shucking corn, helping at hog killing time, washing windows, weeding peanuts and soybeans, and other duties as assigned. I cannot say we always relished performing the chores on the farm, but it was an understood necessity and non-negotiable. As with all rural families, children worked on the farm and our reward was the harvest we all shared. *Pray ye therefore the Lord of the harvest, that he will send forth labourers into his harvest* (Matthew 9:38, KJV).

As the two oldest grandchildren, my sister, Joan Lee and I would crawl out of the low-level bedroom window just before sunup to make sure we were on time to feed the cow who was perpetually named Nellie and the two work mules named Lucky and Millie. When the cow and the mules died, their replacements names remained the same. It was imperative that I rode with Granddaddy on the John Deere tractor or in the buckboard hitched to Lucky, the mule, to feed the hogs...always careful never to venture too close to the sow. "She could be mighty mean if she thought you were going to harm her little ones," Granddaddy would say. One thing was always evident, we all felt accepted and loved by our grandparents.

There was, however, an instance when I was about four or five years old when all the love I felt for them was just not enough. My parents had taken me to visit my grandparents, but this time I did not want to stay. I just wanted to be at home with my mother. Because it was not acceptable for children to have a voice in the decisions that adults made in the early 1950s, I complied in hidden protest. After my parents left and Gramma listened to my bedtime prayers and took the oil lamp out of the room, my real prayer began. "Lord, please send my mother back to get me *tonight or tomorrow morning?*" I do not remember crying or feeling anxious during my prayer. I prayed as if I thoroughly expected God to answer my prayer. In hindsight, I realized I was somehow afraid to voice my objection to my parents but not afraid to let God know I was only giving Him two options to fulfill my prayer request, *"tonight or tomorrow morning."* I went to sleep only to be awakened by my mother before sunrise to take me home. I was thoroughly convinced that God, not only heard me but also loved me enough to do what I asked. I prayed in specifics and He answered in specifics.

Years later, when Mommie and I spoke about this event, she said she felt very unsettled in her spirit after returning home. She had such a strong over-powering sense of urgency to make that 60-mile return trip to the farm despite the objections of my father and Gramma. Mommie told me that *Something told her* to go back to get me. Even my mother did not seem to fully understand her sense of urgency to return, but she chose to follow her "gut" feeling. Because she did, I believed that God truly answers prayer. My mother's *sixth sense* appeared to be functional and working with precision. It was this early encounter with God that set the tone for the remainder of my life and cemented my relationship with the Lord.

There are many stories I remember about Granddaddy, but the one that is most memorable was one he told about growing up very poor and seeking work at twelve years old at the General Store "in town." The white store owner said the only job he could offer was loading customers' buckboards with purchases and it required the ability to lift fifty-pound bags of grain. He said, "If you can do that, you can have the job." Granddaddy knew that because of his small wiry frame, which was like that of a ten-year-old, the expectation was that he would not be able to lift what was so close to his own weight. Though slight of build, Grandaddy obviously had the constitution and faith of Sampson that day and met the challenge to get the job. His earnings went toward the support of his father, Hardy Winfield, his mother, Nettie, and his younger siblings. Between the life I was told about and the life I knew about for my forty-one years at his death, this 5'3' gentleman was a virtual superhero to me. In whatever ways we find happiness for ourselves, we usually want those we care about to enjoy them too. My children, Monica, Donita, and Jaimie received a taste of what I experienced with Granddaddy and Gramma. I made sure they visited and developed their own memories of both of my grandparent's greatness and the love that ran deep in Surry.

My relationship with God was forged in Surry when I was about four or five years old. However, as with many relationships, ours was not always consistently close. I chose to make decisions based on my own mind which appeared to be lost from time to time. I may not always have been listening to God, but He was always mindful of me and not through with me yet. It would be another twelve or thirteen years before I would have another undeniable encounter with Him. God was being His characteristically patient self and He had a plan for me. I was now determined I was ready to yield and follow His lead. *"The Lord is not slow to fulfill his promise as some count slowness, but is patient toward you, not wishing that any should perish, but that all should reach repentance"* (I Peter 3:9, ESV).

In 1963, my husband, James Edwards, III, and I married when he was 21 and I was seventeen. He was an outgoing charismatic guy who instantly stole my heart. Because I was very young and he was very poor, we lived with one or the other of our parents early in our marriage. It was one of those times when we lived with James' parents that I felt an over-whelming sense of despair in our solemn marriage decision. My upper room experience occurred in my attic bedroom one afternoon when I began to talk to God who had been so distant of late because I chose to put Him there. I fell on my knees and prayed for His forgiveness of all my sins. I cried out my frustrations and heartache from the depths of my soul. I don't know how long I had been praying or how long I had been crying those ever-flowing buckets of tears, but suddenly I felt a warm tingling that began from my feet to my head. When I realized I had stopped crying it was now dark. My earlier despair had somehow changed to delight. Now, not only did I feel this new unspeakable joy, but I had a new peace that surpassed all my understanding. I literally "prayed myself happy." *"And the peace of God, which transcends all understanding, will guard your hearts and your minds in Christ Jesus* (Philippians 4:7, NIV).

I left the attic and hurried downstairs to tell the only other person in the house what I had just experienced. It was like fire shut up in my bones... I had to tell somebody. My mother-in-law,

Clarestine, was cooking dinner. I tried to explain my unspeakable joy, but her expression told me I must be babbling or "speaking in tongues" she could not understand. I knew God had once again answered my prayers. All would be well again in my world, even though, I had strayed away from Him. It was clear to me that God forgave and loved me still. *"But His word was in mine heart as a burning fire shut up in my bones"* (Jeremiah 20:9b NIV).

Chapter 10

Great-Great Granddad And Me

I don't remember crying very much when Granddaddy died in 1987, not because I did not love him deeply but because I felt completely confident and comforted knowing he was experiencing the joy of the Lord. At the time, I recalled a portion of Scripture, *"to be absent from the body is to be present with the Lord"* (2 Cor. 5:8, KJV). It seemed appropriate and settling to my spirit.

It was not until 1990, three years after Granddaddy died, that I recollect having a full-blown "grief ambush" moment. While routinely getting ready for church one Sunday morning, Granddaddy crossed my mind and along with many memories of my grandparents, my aunts and uncles, my dad and my siblings on different occasions in Surry. I felt so overwhelmed with grief, I began to cry. I was feeling as if Grandaddy had just died. I wondered how this could be happening. Granddaddy had been dead for three years. Suddenly, a feeling of nervousness came over me. It almost felt as if I might be getting sick. I would describe it as the similar anxiety that occurs when someone verbally gives you a telephone number and you try to retain the number long enough to write it down or put it into your cell phone that you can't seem to find. The Lord was giving me a message and I had to get it right. I frantically searched for something to write on for fear I would forget the words that were forming alarmingly fast in my head.

I finally found a pencil and an old pocket calendar that I had not completely used up. I plopped in a chair in my bedroom and began to write. The words tumbled out so quickly that I used abbreviations I hoped to decipher after the intense outpouring ceased. It was an involuntary response of word flow that was so extreme that I knew it was no longer me who was writing but the Spirit of Almighty God in me.

The result of this epiphany was a poem. As you will recognize in reading the poem, the voice is not mine that addresses my grandfather. It is, however, written in the voice of my grandson, Winfield James Edwards, to his great-great grandfather who he never got a chance to meet. Granddaddy was born in 1892 and died at the age of ninety-five at approximately 5 p.m. on September 12, 1987. Our first grandchild, Winfield, was born at about 5 p.m. on September 13, 1987, approximately twenty-four hours apart. I have no additional explanation for the occurrence I just described except that I experienced a *something told me moment* and now *"I got a praise and I got to let it out."*

Great-Great Granddad and Me

We passed in the halls of eternity,
I recognized him, he recognized me
Not that I knew him in life, you see,
still he left me an heir of great dignity
Born one day too late,
he succumbed to every man's fate
Family will continue to share great tales
of Willie Winfield hoisting barnyard steer.
They'll tell how folks far and wide
loved and respected his god-filled pride.
For him, there was no greater joy than family,
and that includes me.
Downhearted is not in keeping
with this man who is happier being
with God our Father than me.
One day there'll be just us three...
God, Great-Great Grandad and me.
He left me more than can be revealed
He left me the name Winfield.

Chapter 11

James' Something Told Me Moments

The 1980s were filled with great transition and certifiable *something told me moments*. Some of our friends referred to them as certifiably "crazy" moments. These were the years, my husband, James, and I entered into an agreement with my father to purchase the home where I grew up. We had been renting there for about seven years and wanted to purchase a home but knew we had a poor credit history and no money for a down payment and closing costs. Daddy and his second wife, Athylone lived in San Jose, California where Daddy retired from the Navy and from Lockheed Martin Corporation. Seemingly, they had no plans to move back to Virginia and agreed to sell the house to us. In 1983, James accepted his call to preach and was licensed by our church, Historic

First Baptist Church on Bute Street, Norfolk, Virginia. He counseled with our pastor, Rev. LaVert Taylor, who left the church before licensing him. However, our new pastor, Dr. Robert G. Murray, counseled and licensed him to preach and our ministry journey began. In that same year, my husband told me that the Lord spoke to him and said to resign from his $26,000/year salaried position at the local newspaper, The Virginian Pilot and Ledger Star. My first thought was, "What do you mean, quit your job and start a daycare business?" James did not say, *something told him* to quit his job and open a daycare located at our home we just bought from my father. James' love for Christ and maturity of faith, at this point in his life, let him know who was really speaking to him. Who was I to challenge what James said God told him? I told my husband, "Just don't wait until I'm fifty to start a business."

My husband had an education degree in Physical Education but neither of us had daycare experience. We could not seem to agree on a name for our business and Joan Lee suggested, JaDe which were the first two letters in James and my first name. We opened JaDe Family Daycare for business in 1983 with one unsalaried employee, my sister, Joan Lee, and two tuition free students enrolled... my daughter, Jaimie, and Joan's son, Duward, Jr. It was time for our two oldest daughters to go college and suddenly they could attend because our reduced income made them eligible for financial aid and college grants. I continued to work full time at Sentara Norfolk General Hospital, and part-time at the JaDe Family Daycare until 1986.

While walking from the parking lot to my job at the hospital in the spring of 1986, a thought formed in my mind, *"You will not be working here when it gets cold."* Now this was the same job I knew the Lord had given me in 1973 and *His still small voice* was letting me know, it was time to go. By the end of August, I submitted my resignation with no other job in sight. But just as God did not give specifics about leaving the job, He also never told me to look for another one, either.

Our friends and family were perplexed as they stood by and helplessly watched us make decisions that threw us into tumultuous life changes. Within a few months, our lives had completely transformed from a stable income with the benefits of medical insurance to a below poverty existence and no plan "B." We fell behind on all payments on bills and mortgage to my father. People who were close to us knew we were struggling but the community saw us smiling as if all was well. James managed our business with a tender heart towards financially strapped families and those dealing with family turmoil. We took children with us to church when parents were extremely late, nursed them when they were sick (separated from others), and fed them, like they were our children. I believe someone was watching us and God was touching hearts because someone anonymously sent us individual cashier's checks in the same amount in each of our names. Although we ardently searched to find the person, to this day, we do not know who this generous soul was. We do remember it as a gift from God with gratitude.

It is only in reviewing the past that we see how the Holy Spirit intervened in our lives in preparation for *"the substance of things hoped for and the evidence of things not seen" (Hebrews 11:1, KJV).* The following chronology of events will help clarify the certifiable.

- 1983 – James was licensed to preach

- 1983 – James resigned from his job and opened JaDe Family Daycare

- 1985 – James enrolled in seminary at Virginia Union University's Samuel Dewitt Proctor School of Theology weekend master's program in Richmond, Virginia.

- 1986 – James accepted a pastoral call to First Baptist Church Orlando, Suffolk, Virginia

- 1986 – I resigned from my job at Sentara Norfolk General Hospital

- 1986 and 1987 – Daughters Monica entered Tidewater Community College and Donita enrolled at Virginia State University

- 1986 – One month after resigning from my job at Sentara Norfolk General Hospital, Drs. Benjamin and Sylvia Laremont called my husband to ask him if I could come to work for them. I agreed to work for them with the understanding that I would be off every Friday at 12 Noon while James was in seminary.

Following the lead of the Holy Spirit is not easy or comfortable sometimes. My husband was steadfast about hearing from God, regardless of what it looked like to others. I could not, I would not go against what God was speaking to Him. The critical correlation of each event in isolation has little or no meaning as to the outcome. However, when examining them contextually, the sheer magnitude of the orchestration of the Holy Spirit cannot be denied.

After James accepted his call to preach, the concept of starting a daycare business began to form in his mind. He could not start the daycare business unless he resigned from his position at the Newspaper. He could not go to seminary unless he did the first two things. I had to resign from my position at Sentara Norfolk General so that when the Laremonts called to offer me a job, I would be able to work but also ask for a half day off to supervise the daycare business. Our two oldest daughters would never have been able to attend college with little assistance from their parents because before these life changes, we made too much money.

We would never have been able to continue the business without bringing our home up to city building code standards. God *sent* an unlikely contractor with an equally unlikely personality to beautifully design a functional daycare and family home dwelling over a three-year period. Jerry Cross blessed us beyond measure and many times waited on his payments. At any other point in our lives, we would never have entered a contract with a white guy, wearing an open shirt, and sporting several large gold chains. He was a Kenny Rogers look-a-like driving a black Cadillac convertible, advertising his Triangle Builders contract business in a Black neighborhood. Our paths were destined to overlap.

We became very well acquainted with Jerry and shared our testimony of God's intervention in our lives, our faith, and our aspirations with him. Sometime later after the projects were completed, Jerry Cross came to visit us. He let us know he was moving from the area to North Carolina and that he had accepted Jesus Christ as his Savior...and here we thought we just needed a contractor.

Finally, a young man named Kenneth Royster came to our door selling insurance in the midst of our building renovations. Ken was just starting out in the insurance business. I cannot even remember why we took time to listen to his spiel except, *something* urged me to do so. He presented such a convincing sale's pitch about the benefit of having an accidental death policy that we bought one from him. Thank God, we did not have to use the policy. Little did we know that we were destined to become conjoined with this future financial mastermind and great man of God and his future family. Since those faithful years, Ken has grown his faith and his financial business exponentially. We realize that without him in our lives for so many years, we would not be in a position to experience retirement freedom. Now these are certifiable *something told me* moments. The 1980s found us in financial strains, but we were trusting God to work it out. ...and did He ever?

The needle now appeared to be moving me towards a greater awareness and acceptance of my own *sixth sense*. It was becoming clear that the *sixth sense* was more than just a chance occurrence. I also did not seem to use my old quote as often, "I don't want it, you can have it, it's too much for me." Instead of "fighting the feeling" I was learning to "go with the flow."

Chapter 12

Looking For Miss Annie

Confirmation for me having the *sixth sense* unexpectedly presented itself in the spring or early summer of 1983. Thoughts about a woman I had known from my youth, kept coming to my mind. It had been nearly twenty years since I had seen or even heard anyone speak of her. It would have seemed more likely for me to think about her daughter, Mary Mebane, who had been my mother's best friend in the latter years of Mommie's life. I remember that Mary was three or four years younger than my mother and we had been neighbors until she divorced and moved in with her mother, Mrs. Annie Evans and her husband, "Buster," in Norfolk. Mary never had children and became a staple in our home. She seemed to enjoy our busy household of kids, vagrants, and temporary live-ins. She and my mother had a special bond, as Mary had a way of disagreeing with Mommie about something and remain still close friends. When my father received orders to move to Long Island, NY in 1963, it was no surprise and seemed natural that Mary packed up and moved with them. She lived with my parents until the Navy's new orders directed him to move to Minneapolis, Minnesota. Mary declared Long Island was as far as she was going. She had settled in with new friends and a job she enjoyed. Mary and my parents remained in close contact until Mommie's death in 1971.

I don't remember seeing or really thinking about Mary's mother again until 1983. At first, it felt like a hint of wondering about her and how she was doing. As the days progressed, the hint turned into a full-fledged hunt for Miss Annie. Each morning, I seemed to wake up with her on my mind and what I could do to find her. It occurred to me that Miss Annie's cousin, Naomi Whitehurst, her husband Walter, and Naomi's sister, Shirley Allmond, might know where I could find Miss Annie. When I visited Naomi, she had lost contact with her cousin and only gave a vague possible location of some apartments on Granby Street in Norfolk. After church on the following Sunday, I asked my sister, Joan Lee, to go with me to one of many sets of apartments on Granby Street. We went from one section to another looking for Miss Annie's name to be posted on one of the apartment access panels so she could buzz us in. We left the complex feeling a bit disillusioned. I went home and spoke to the Lord out loud, "I have done all that I can to find Miss Annie. If I am supposed to find her, you show me." At 5:45 a.m. the next morning, I arrived at Sentara Norfolk General Hospital where I worked as a telephone operator. This Monday morning was no different than any other and since the telephone traffic was light, I leisurely perused the overnight patient roster when one name seemed to lift right off the page. Amazingly, the person for whom I had been looking was a few floors up from where I worked every day. As soon as one of the other operators could relieve me, I made my way upstairs to see Miss. Annie. I tried to explain to her how I had been looking for her for weeks and I could not explain why. I remember her talking about my mother and how highly she thought of her and how Mommie was such a wonderful friend to her daughter, Mary, who still lived and worked on Long Island. Miss Annie also said she always held Daddy, my siblings, and me in the highest regard. She said she always thought there was something special about me and knew I would grow up to be a wonderful person. Miss Annie shared that I had also been on her mind recently and she too had been wondering how each of us were doing. After our meeting, I visited Miss Annie each day and promised to keep in touch with her when she was released from the hospital. A week later, she was released and, as promised, I visited her apartment on Granby Street and realized why I could not find her name on my initial quest. Miss Annie said when she moved into the apartment, she purposefully left the previous tenants name on the access panel. She thought it would be an additional security measure. Joan Lee and I remembered going to that apartment, but perhaps she was waiting for me to find her at the hospital. Over the next several weeks I visited Miss Annie several times and got reacquaint with Mary who came from Long Island to care for her mom. We laughed and shared many fond memories of days long gone by. Sadly, Miss Annie died of congestive heart failure after being at home for a few weeks.

You might be wondering the same thing I have wondered for many years since my *something told me moment* with Mrs. Annie Evans. Why was she on my mind so heavily? What was supposed to be accomplished in locating her? The Lord did what I asked and showed me her name on the hospital roster. When I first received the "hint" from God, Miss. Annie was not even in the hospital... so why the urgency to find her? After much wrestling about the matter, I remembered the Alfred Lloyd Tennyson quote, "Ours not to reason why, ours but to do and die," which seemed to capture the rationale for my quandary. I cannot claim to know why it was important to find Miss Annie, at that particular time. I did not come away with some profound tidbit of wisdom or insight I would not otherwise have. Yet, I believe the Spirit of Christ moved me to be where she was because it was what Miss Annie wanted or needed before closing her eyes for the last time. It was not only the last time I saw Miss Annie but also the last time I saw Mary who returned to Long Island without a trace. For many years she was a big part of our family. I think of her from time to time with fondness and many uproariously funny stories. Although I tried to get her to share her contact information before leaving Virginia, she would not. I believe we are all on a journey where we intersect with others by Divine design...only to reconnect as the Holy Spirit orchestrates until our assignments are completed. When the Spirit moves, it is not for us to question but by faith accept the assignment so that His will be done.

Chapter 13

It's Never Too Late To Be On Assignment

As believers, we must be cognizant that each of us is always on assignment. Consistently seeking His will means our antennae are always up and attuned to His Voice. Our instincts should routinely be on high alert. God is seeking for his people to put Him above all else because our Heavenly Father is not influenced by the outward appearance but by the inward articulation of the heart. *"The Lord does not look at the things people look at. People look at the outward appearance, but the Lord looks at the heart" (I Samuel 16:7b, NIV).* We are anointed, as His children, not by meaningless ceremony but by a divine power that is omniscient, omnipotent, and omnipresent. He has imbued us with His Spirit and as such, we are to operate under His sovereignty.

Instinct: The Power to Unleash Your Inborn Drive by Bishop T.D. Jakes posits this truth:

"Not one of us is born without instincts. A person is more likely to be born without sight than to be born without insight. In fact, many of my blind friends rely upon insight. All of us have internal senses beyond the physical with which we can better determine what's next, what's safe, or even what's right. Our instincts speak to us daily, prompting us to pay attention, to listen more carefully, to sidestep danger, and to seize an opportunity."

Being on assignment also means we are on a mission. Through the ages countless souls have sought to answer the age-old question of life. Is this all there is? What is the meaning and the purpose of life? As we read the book of Ecclesiastes, we learn that King Solomon wrote it because of his intense desire to know and understand the meaning of life and his wise analysis also relevant for us today. Chapter 1 begins with the words, *"Meaningless"* or *"Vanity."* In other words, the Scripture is saying life is useless...it is pointless. Solomon rightly noted that the sun rises and sets, tides ebb and flow, seasons change, and everything seems to just repeat itself generation after generation. However, by the time we get to chapter 3, Solomon affirms with great wisdom that everything God made is beautiful in its time...in its season. God has purposed our lives from beginning to end and in our season, *we are to be happy and find joy in doing good while we live.* Life is God's gift to us.

The answer to our reason for existing is the same as King Solomon's answer. The meaning of life rests upon us responding in obedience to the same still small Voice that speaks through the *sixth sense, the feeling, the sight, intuition, ESP, instincts or sense of urgency, that prompting, that something told me.* It is the spiritual sense of connection to something grander, bigger, more important than us. We find meaning when we seek and find our purpose and our goals. Everyone has a purpose for living. *"The grass withers and the flower fades, But the word of our God stands forever (Isaiah 40:8, NAS).*

My love for God has not diminished or faded as His word remains relevant in my life. I continue to seek His grace and favor for the new ventures, new assignments ahead. I have learned to allow the Holy Spirit to serve as *"a lamp unto my feet and a light unto my path"* (Ps. 119:105, KJV).

God continues to light my path even though I have fewer years ahead of me than those behind me. Yet, I am encouraged in that *"The faithful love of the LORD never ends! His mercies never cease.*

Great is his faithfulness; his mercies begin afresh each morning" (Lamentations 3:22-23, NLT).

Through the *something told* me vignettes and remembrances I have shared, I can say with utmost confidence how by God's grace this *sixth sense* has propelled, pushed, urged me from the time I was about five years old, through my teens, early adulthood, and now middle age. It is so important to understand that His lamp continues to light our path until the Lord's will for our life is done. It is equally important to remember that it is never too late to begin a new chapter or accept a new assignment.

There are many examples of God's people learning/starting new adventures or major initiatives in life after 50. Moses, the Law Giver, was 80 years old and Aaron, his brother was 83 when they spoke to Pharaoh, demanding that he let God's people go free (Exodus 5:1). Abraham was

100 and his wife Sarah was 90 and barren, too old to conceive a child but she believed God and conceived (Hebrews 11:4). In our recent history, many of us may remember Julia Childs, the celebrity chef who at 50 wrote her first cookbook. Ray Kroc was a milkshake device salesman before he founded the McDonald's Golden Arches at 52, and Harlan Sanders purchased a franchise at 62 and became Colonel Sanders of Kentucky Fried Chicken fame. I took these examples seriously and was undaunted in what I knew God had for me in my middle years.

For 30 years, intermittently, I attended Tidewater Community College or other institution of higher learning to earn a number of certifications. Each time one of my children or my husband or grandson decided to advance their education, I deferred my dreams. But in June 2000, my husband brought home a brochure from the annual Hampton University Ministers' Conference about a new accredited pilot degree program in Religious Studies. After reviewing the program, I felt compelled to complete the information and seek admission within three weeks. The feeling of urgency was intense. I knew this new assignment would lead to the fulfillment of a personal goal I had sought for thirty years. I took my transcript with thirty credits and met with the director of the program, Dr. Calvin Sydnor, and was informed by letter I had been accepted into the program.

I could not believe I was finally going to be working toward a degree from Hampton University (HU). I would join our HU family history along with my great Aunt Dorothy Leigh (Mainor) Maynor and Joan Lee. I cried with joy through Old Testament and New Testament theology classes and praised God with song and praise in the midnight hour through pastoral counseling. I cried for so much more than a family legacy…I cried because of the joy of connecting my studies to my faith. I saw the Old Testament Major and Minor Prophets with fresh eyes. The study of Greek and the humanities enhanced my scholarly views that informed new sermons and new perspectives on life. I read, I wrote, and I researched until James worried about me pushing too hard for my health. God had given me the desire of my heart and graduation was in sight. My bonus blessing was that I completed my religious study degree free of debt. James' and my combined salaries and our debt ratio never aligned with the cost of tuition, yet we did not experience budget pressure nor miss a beat giving our tithes and offerings to God. I believe that God arranged for me to receive this degree in His time frame from beginning to end including a "paid in full" receipt.

It was hard work filled with many challenges to finish but the Lord opened a clear path to Hampton

University to receive my Bachelor of Arts in Religious Studies and I bear witness that according to Matthew 11:30, KJV, *"My yoke is easy and My burden is light."* I graduated Magna Cum Laude in 2004 when I was 58 years old. My fellow graduate in the pilot program was Rev. Michael Dyson, not the renowned preacher, professor, author, and radio personality. My classmate became the pastor of Sharon Seventh Day Adventist Church in Baltimore, Maryland. Rev. Dyson and I both understood that it was not by chance that the two of us were the pioneers in this pilot program. We were the first students to complete requirements for an online degree not previously offered by HU. Today, seminarians can earn a master's or doctorate degree using this non-traditional online medium. Greater, bigger, more important things were to be accomplished in becoming students in this pilot program. Michael and I had unknowingly become trailblazers for Hampton University but more importantly, Champions for Christ. As students in this degree program, our unifying principle was to walk worthy of our calling to ministry. *"Therefore, the prisoner of the Lord, beseech you that ye walk worthy of the vocation wherewith ye are called, With all lowliness and meekness, with longsuffering, forbearing one another in love (Ephesians 4:1-2, KJV).*

God wants each of us to continue seeking the meaning and purpose of life wherever it leads. I would submit to you that no other person can provide a particular design or give specific instruction as to the direction and scope of your journey, but you. What led me to this place was my *sixth sense, mother wit, the urgency, the site, ESP, a feeling, the sight or the spirit.* In this instance, the terminology is not as important because my motives, my values, and my beliefs are based on my meticulously ordered steps by my Father in heaven. As Christians we are not only striving to go to heaven, although that will be our destination as believers in Jesus Christ, but we should be striving to please God and bless others.

We have a limited time and opportunity on this earth to pursue our divine destiny. There is no roadmap, no crystal ball, no book, no search engine, sage, philosopher, theorist, or other human entity who can give specific instructions as to your journey or my journey. I urge you to keep your spiritual eyes wide open for the unfolding revelations of God. Biblical reminders of basic truths can help us stay focused on our real purpose in life which is to be magnets for Christ, connecting others, as Jesus said to his disciples, *"This is My commandment, that you love one another, just as I have loved you (John 15:12, NASB). The sixth sense* and the other five are to be used harmoniously and in sync with God's will.

I would remind you of my observation when I was a child regarding the *sixth sense*, "Whatever it is, I don't want it." I saw this *"feeling"* as something to be feared. I saw the expression of people who experienced it as painful, anxiety ridden. I never seemed to hear anything positive, exciting, or enlightening about having these *something told me moments* manifest themselves. As far as I was concerned, it was a foretaste of an unchangeable event that had not happened yet and no way of improving the outcome. I did not understand what purpose there was in having this *"mother wit."* What purpose could it possibly serve? As a result, I determined, out of my own limited understanding and fear that the *sixth sense* must be a bad thing. In my case, I did not fear my family members, the vessels through whom the *sixth sense* was demonstrated, but I feared their state of worry and alarm. No one every explained it... nor did I ever ask. Each family member, my grandmother, my mother, and my sister seemed to just accept from generation to generation. It is amazing what a bit of maturity can help settle in our own mind. My paternal grandmother, Naomi Brown Winfield, would probably have said it like this, "Just keep living...you'll understand it by and by."

Chapter 14

Let the Spirit Lead You; God Is Still Speaking

"But when He, the Spirit of truth, comes, He will guide you into all the truth; for He will not speak on His own initiative, but whatever He hears, He will speak; and He will disclose to you what is to come" *(John 16:13, NASB).* This scriptural background conveys that Christ completed His work on earth, after the resurrection, and referred the disciples to the coming of the Holy Spirit by whom they would receive power. In addition, we understand that Jesus promised that the Spirit would come to lead, guide, and direct the disciples to carry out the mission Jesus shared as the gospel of salvation. I like to think of it in terms of Jesus passing the baton and trusting the runner (Holy Spirit) to run the race in His stead and cross victoriously at the finish line.

Christ referred to the Holy Spirit as the *Spirit of Truth*. It is this Spirit that would be with the disciples and remain in the world leading us to not just know the truth, but search and know the deep things of God. He would show them things to come. The Spirit is one with the Father and the Son and has been given authority to operate in their name. Our *sixth sense* which was given to us by God at the beginning, is activated, developed, and manifested in us by the Holy Spirit. It is by this Spirit that we receive guidance, instruction, power, and comfort that comes from Christ... to His disciples...to you and me.

"Beloved, do not believe every spirit, but test the spirits to see whether they are from God, because many false prophets have gone out into the world. By this you know the Spirit of God: every spirit that confesses that Jesus Christ has come in the flesh is from God" (I Jn. 4:1-3). You might be

wondering how to go about testing the spirit by the spirit. Remember, the Spirit of God already knows and connects with our spirit. God wants us to try...to test...to recognize His Spirit. I tested God at five years old and gave Him the option to have my mother return to get me from my grandparent's home either tonight or tomorrow morning. I tried Him to see if He would hear my prayer and respond to what I asked. I heard in Sunday school that whatever I would ask of the Father in Jesus' name He would do it. I possessed a child's mustard seed faith and because of it the Lord responded with a "watermelon" blessing.

When we are in right relationship with Christ, He can use us for His glory. Jesus entrusted the Holy Spirit to finish the good and perfect work, He began with the Twelve. Likewise, he entrusts believers to continue the work of salvation. How will you know which spirit is speaking, God or Satan? *"My sheep know my voice and a stranger; they will not follow (John 10:4-5, KJV).*

Think with me about how we trusted our parents when we were little. If we ventured too far from them while shopping, we called out for them. They immediately knew our voices above the din of other shoppers. When they responded, we immediately recognized their voices and began to move towards it. God comes to each of us in different ways. He may come in a fleeting thought in anticipation of some unknown event or it may be for a moment or over an extended period of time.

Trust in a relationship is not always easily formed. Relationships can be tested and proven periodically, much like the Spirit. This relationship between God and man is exceptionally one-sided and sometimes to our chagrin. There is always a consequence we must pay for disobedience. Our human nature dictates that we are often easily distracted and by the same nature rather fickle and unreliable. We tend not to do what we promised while God, according to His divine nature remains faithful. The amazing, wonderful, and extraordinary blessing is that even when we mess up, God never fails or falls short of His promises.

The Bible is the divinely inspired, infallible, inerrant word of God. Reading it consistently helps keep us in tune and in touch with our Creator. We need only to be willing vessels when that *sense of urgency* or *uneasiness*, or *anxiety* manifests itself. Pray for understanding and guidance as to what you are to do. The Holy Spirit will always connect with the spirit within you and instruct you in every way.

Since I began writing this book in 2015, the United States singularly holds the dreaded distinction for highest case numbers for novel Corona Virus in this global pandemic, more than

10.2 million at this writing. Not since the Spanish flu in 1918 have we seen such astronomical loss of life. More than 240,000 lives have been lost between January and November 2020 due to Covid-19. This number of deaths is four times the number of American lives lost in the eleven years during the Vietnam War. God is still speaking and Instructing us, even in the midst of a pandemic for which there is no vaccine or treatment.

In March 2020, I came across a portion of a dream, I dated, January 12, 2018. In the dream I could see scrambled letters hovering above me. I strained to see the letters clearly, but they were blurred, uneven, and unrecognizable. Slowly the letters took form and it read, "He came and pestilence was with Him."

I recognized the reference to Psalm 91 and when I read the Psalm again, the Lord led me to the fifth verse that reads, *"Thou shalt not be afraid for the terror by night; nor for the arrow that flieth by day; Nor for the pestilence that walketh in darkness; nor for the destruction that wasteth at noonday. A thousand shall fall at thy side, and ten thousand at thy right hand; but it shall not come nigh thee (Ps 91:5-7 KJV).* There was no pestilence (novel corona virus) in 2018. Why did I have the dream and why did I write it in a journal? I believe the Lord knew I would need a point of tangible reference as well as personal reassurance because I could then speak peace to myself and others during a worldwide storm of death and disease, *"it shall not come nigh thee..."* For me this served as another confirmation that God still speaks, and I am still listening.

God has not forgotten nor is He looking the other way while we struggle in this world. He sends messages to us, sometimes before an event happens. He is still speaking. I am positive that my family and I are not the only servants through whom the Spirit is speaking. I am humbled by the gift and the Giver of the *sixth sense. "Every good gift and every perfect present comes from heaven; it comes down from God, the Creator of the heavenly lights, who does not change or cause darkness by turning"* (James 1:17, GNT).

Within Christian context, the believer's desire to gain a deeper relationship with Christ often seems far away and unattainable. If you are wondering why God's desire for our lives is not clearer, easier to understand and succinct, you are not alone. My perspective is that God knows His creation better than His creation know our selves. People tend to take for granted those things received from God with little or no effort on their part. We sometimes see the blessings of a spouse, children, home, job, love, and acceptance as what is expected and therefore attribute less value to them. Value is assigned only when we receive our reward at the conclusion...when the pain, the struggle, bitter defeat, heartbreaking efforts, fear of failure and the unknown variables of life have been endured. Realizing we have the gifts because of God's favor on us and not because of our own efforts is a step that leads us to begin operating in the Spirit. To know the will of God for our lives requires that we have a total commitment to do so in heart, mind, body, soul, and strength. Jesus said, *"You shall love the LORD your God with all your heart, with all your soul, with all your strength, and with all your mind..." (Luke 10:27, NKJV).*

The *sixth sense* was designed to completely meld with the Holy Spirit to bring God's plan of salvation into fruition. As you learn to trust God's process you become fine-tuned to hearing Him speak. With the wholehearted innocence of a child's prayer, I expected a loving God to fully answer my prayer. In total surrender, God gave a teen-aged bride peace that passed all understanding in an upper room encounter. Finding Uncle Howard caused my grandmother's heart, mind, body, soul and strength to work in tandem until her assignment was accomplished.

As believers, I pray we can "touch and agree" that the *sight, the feeling, mother wit, the urgency, the sixth sense* is a blessing. This *sixth sense* was given before we were born so that we might live out our lives devoted to God and dedicated to others. Knowing what I know now, I can never again, in good conscience say, *"Something told me"* when experiencing the *sixth sense* operating in my life. No longer should we give honor to some unknown, mysterious entity called *"Something"* when we have had an encounter with God. The mystery has been solved, the unknown has been identified, and the dark has been brought to the light. We can glory in our unrestrained praise to

God, for it is He who told us, urged us, stirred us into action with understanding. It is the Holy Spirit who speaks and gives us utterance, not *"Something."*

My prayer is that you have become more open-minded about someone you know who displays the *sixth sense*. I pray that any fear of this gift has been removed. I ask God that if you have been enlightened and enlivened regarding your own blessed spiritual insight, you will allow the Spirit to guide and direct. Share your testimony freely and let God deal with the naysayers and skeptics.

May God grant that you received in your reading what God intended in my writing!

In Christ,

I am,

Love,

Rev. Dee

Biographical Sketch
Rev. Delores Winfield Edwards

Rev. Edwards is an ordained associate minister at Historic First Baptist Church, Norfolk, VA. She is one of the co-founders and facilitator of its grief counseling group. She earned a Bachelor of Arts degree in Religious Studies, graduating Cum Laude, from Hampton University and a Master of Arts Degree in Urban Education Community Counseling from Norfolk State University. She is co-author of a book titled, *Then There Were Three: Wake Up to the Ministry Call.* She has been married for 57 years to Rev. Dr. James Edwards, III and they have three daughters, two sons-in-law, eight grandchildren and two great-grandsons. Rev. Dee's favorite Scripture: "When my heart is overwhelmed: lead me to a rock that is higher than I" (Ps. 61:2b, KJV).

Contact Information:

Rev. Delores Winfield Edwards
Email: deeedwards0413@gmail.com
Telephone: 757-338-6887

Other Titles by Jade Publishing

Then There Were Three: Wake up to the Ministry Call
ISBN: 978-0-692-39446-5

The Dark Side of Norfolk: Through God's Eyes
ISBN: 978-0-9992591-0-8

And What More Shall I Say?
ISBN: 978-0-9992591-1-5

My Name Is Blake Edwards
ISBN: 978-0-9992591-2-2

*The Man You Are Trying to Marry Is Not Your
Husband: A Message for Single Women Pursuing the
Call to Destiny*
(e-book)

www.ingramcontent.com/pod-product-compliance
Lightning Source LLC
Chambersburg PA
CBHW071554040426
42452CB00008B/1167